A GLIMPSE OF FRUITS

A Detailed Information Of Fruits

A Glimpse Of Fruits

ISBN 9798846081093
Imprint: Independently published

mohdathar145@gmail.com

APPLE

An apple is an edible fruit produced by an apple tree (Malus domestica). Apple trees are cultivated worldwide and are the most widely grown species in the genus Malus. The tree originated in Central Asia, where its wild ancestor, Malus sieversii, is still found today. Apples have been grown for thousands of years in Asia and Europe and were brought to North America by European colonists. Apples have religious and mythological significance in many cultures, including Norse, Greek, and European Christian tradition.

APRICOT

These small fleshy fruits are closely related to peaches and plums. The skin of an apricot is typically yellow and orange with a splash of red, while the fruit on the inside ranges from yellow to orange. Apricots can be enjoyed fresh or in their dried form.

Notable source of dietary fiber.
Outstanding source of vitamin A and vitamin C.
Provides calcium for healthy bones.

AVOCADO

Avocados have swept the nation in recent years. These nutrient dense fruits can be consumed by themselves, smashed into guacamole or even used in chocolate desserts. It's easy to see why people love them – avocados are packed with nutrients!

Contains high amounts of healthy fats.
Good source of fiber.
Rich in protein and potassium.

BANANA

A banana is an elongated, edible fruit - botanically a berry - produced by several kinds of large herbaceous flowering plants in the genus Musa. In some countries, bananas used for cooking may be called "plantains", distinguishing them from dessert bananas. The fruit is variable in size, color, and firmness, but is usually elongated and curved, with soft flesh rich in starch covered with a rind, which may be green, yellow, red, purple, or brown when ripe. The fruits grow upward in clusters near the top of the plant.

BLACKBERRIES

The blackberry is an edible fruit produced by many species in the genus Rubus in the family Rosaceae, hybrids among these species within the subgenus Rubus, and hybrids between the subgenera Rubus and Idaeobatus.

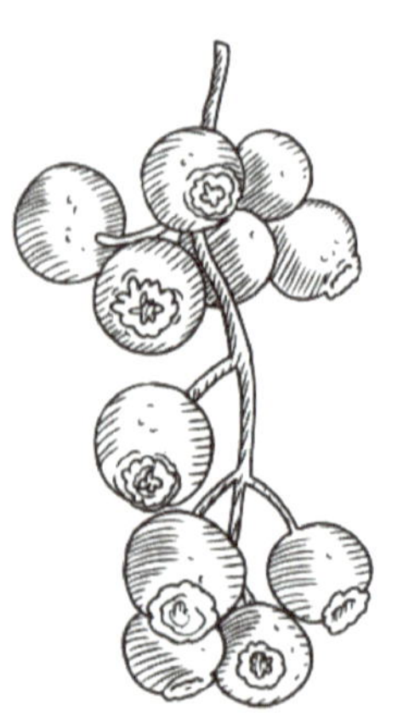

BLUEBERRY

Blueberries are small dark blue or purple berries that have low sugar content despite tasting so sweet. These tasty little fruits are often baked into desserts, added to breakfasts or enjoyed alone. Often labeled a superfood, blueberries are a great addition to your diet because of their numerous health benefits.

Rich in vitamin K and vitamin C.
Outstanding source of manganese.
High in antioxidants, particularly flavonoids.

CHERRY

Though often associated with berries, these sweet red fruits are classified as drupes. Fresh cherries can be cooked with red meats, used as a garnish for desserts and of course, eaten as a fresh snack. These low-calorie fruits are packed with nutrients.

Excellent source of vitamin A and vitamin C.
Potassium-rich food.
Low on the glycemic index, making them better for blood sugar.

COCONUT

The coconut tree (Cocos nucifera) is a member of the palm tree family (Arecaceae) and the only living species of the genus Cocos. The term "coconut" (or the archaic "cocoanut") can refer to the whole coconut palm, the seed, or the fruit, which botanically is a drupe, not a nut. The name comes from the old Portuguese word coco, meaning "head" or "skull", after the three indentations on the coconut shell that resemble facial features. They are ubiquitous in coastal tropical regions and are a cultural icon of the tropics.

CUSTARD APPLE

Custard apple is a common name for a fruit, and the tree which bears it, *Annona reticulata*.
The fruits vary in shape, heart-shaped, spherical, oblong or irregular. The size ranges from 7 to 12 cm (2.8 to 4.7 in), depending on the cultivar. When ripe, the fruit is brown or yellowish, with red highlights and a varying degree of reticulation, depending again on the variety. The flesh varies from juicy and very aromatic to hard with an astringent taste. The flavor is sweet and pleasant, akin to the taste of 'traditional' custard.

The custard apple is native to the Americas, but has been found on the island of Timor as early as 1000 CE

DATE PALM

Phoenix dactylifera, commonly known as date or date palm, is a flowering plant species in the palm family, Arecaceae, cultivated for its edible sweet fruit called dates. The species is widely cultivated across northern Africa, the Middle East, and South Asia, and is naturalized in many tropical and subtropical regions worldwide. Dactylifera is the type species of genus Phoenix, which contains 12-19 species of wild date palms.

DRAGON FRUIT

A pitaya (/pɪˈtaɪ.ə/) or pitahaya (/ˌpɪtə ˈhaɪ.ə/) is the fruit of several different cactus species indigenous to the Americas.[Pitaya usually refers to fruit of the genus Stenocereus, while pitahaya or dragon fruit refers to fruit of the genus Selenicereus (formerly Hylocereus), both in the family Cactaceae. Dragon fruit is cultivated in Peru, Mexico, South Asia, Southeast Asia, East Asia, the United States, the Caribbean, Australia, Mesoamerica and throughout tropical and subtropical regions of the world.

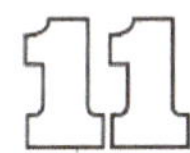

FIG

The fig is the edible fruit of Ficus carica, a species of small tree in the flowering plant family Moraceae. Native to the Mediterranean and western Asia, it has been cultivated since ancient times and is now widely grown throughout the world, both for its fruit and as an ornamental plant. Ficus carica is the type species of the genus Ficus, containing over 800 tropical and subtropical plant species.

GOOSEBERRY

Gooseberries are small green berries that are quite tart in flavor. They are commonly used in sauces and desserts. Fresh gooseberries are only available for a few weeks during the summer but people enjoy canned gooseberries year round.

Provide half of the recommended daily amount of vitamin C.
Good source of both soluble and insoluble fiber.
High vitamin A content.

GRAPES

A grape is a fruit, botanically a berry, of the deciduous woody vines of the flowering plant genus Vitis.
Grapes can be eaten fresh as table grapes, used for making wine, jam, grape juice, jelly, grape seed extract, vinegar, and grape seed oil, or dried as raisins, currants and sultanas. Grapes are a non-climacteric type of fruit, generally occurring in clusters.

GUAVA

Guava (/ˈgwɑːvə/) is a common tropical fruit cultivated in many tropical and subtropical regions. The common guava Psidium guajava (lemon guava, apple guava) is a small tree in the myrtle family (Myrtaceae), native to Mexico, Central America, the Caribbean and northern South America. The name guava is also given to some other species in the genus Psidium such as strawberry guava (Psidium cattleyanum) and to the pineapple guava, Feijoa sellowiana. In 2019, 55 million tonnes of guavas were produced worldwide, led by India with 45% of the total. Botanically, guavas are berries.

HONEYDEW MELON

Honeydew melon, or honeymelon, is a fruit that belongs to the melon species cucumis melo (muskmelon).
The sweet flesh of honeydew is typically light green, while its skin has a white-yellow tone. Its size and shape are similar to that of its relative, the cantaloupe.
Honeydew melon is available worldwide and can be eaten by itself or used in desserts, salads, snacks and soups.
Though its greatest appeal may be its flavor, honeydew is also nutritious and may provide several benefits.

KIWIFRUIT

Kiwifruit (often shortened to kiwi in North America and continental Europe) or Chinese gooseberry is the edible berry of several species of woody vines in the genus Actinidia. The most common cultivar group of kiwifruit (Actinidia deliciosa 'Hayward') is oval, about the size of a large hen's egg: 5-8 centimetres (2-3 inches) in length and 4.5-5.5 cm (1+3/4-2+1/4 in) in diameter. It has a thin, fuzzy, fibrous, tart but edible light brown skin and light green or golden flesh with rows of tiny, black, edible seeds. The fruit has a soft texture with a sweet and unique flavour.

KUMQUAT

Kumquats (/ˈkʌmkwɒt/; Chinese: 金桔), or cumquats in Australian English, are a group of small fruit-bearing trees in the flowering plant family Rutaceae. Their taxonomy is disputed. They were previously classified as forming the now-historical genus Fortunella or placed within Citrus, sensu lato. Different classifications have alternatively assigned them to anywhere from a single species, C. japonica, to numerous species representing each cultivar. Recent genomic analysis would define three pure species, Citrus hindsii, C. margarita and C. crassifolia, with C. x japonica being a hybrid of the last two.

LONGAN

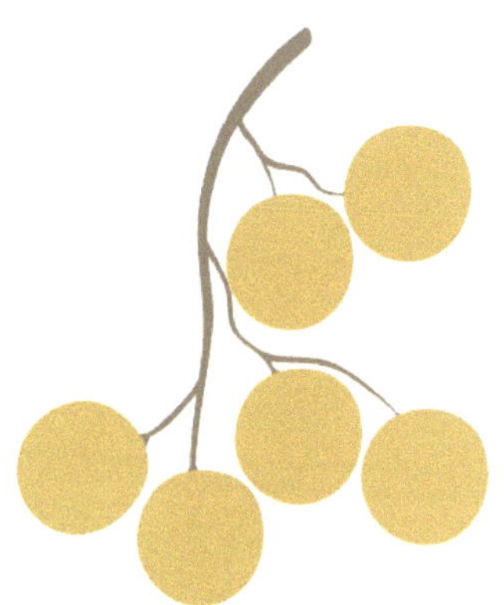

Dimocarpus longan, commonly known as the longan (/ˈlɒŋɡən/), is a tropical tree species that produces edible fruit. It is one of the better-known tropical members of the soapberry family Sapindaceae, to which the lychee and rambutan also belong. The fruit of the longan is similar to that of the lychee, but less aromatic in taste. It is native to tropical Asia and China.

LYCHEE

Lychee, (Litchi chinensis), also spelled litchi or lichi, evergreen tree of the soapberry family (Sapindaceae), grown for its edible fruit. Lychee is native to Southeast Asia and has been a favourite fruit of the Cantonese since ancient times. The fruit is usually eaten fresh but can also be canned or dried. The flavour of the fresh pulp is aromatic and musky, and the dried pulp is acidic and very sweet.

MANGO

A mango is an edible stone fruit produced by the tropical tree Mangifera indica which is believed to have originated in the region between northwestern Myanmar, Bangladesh, and northeastern India. M. indica has been cultivated in South and Southeast Asia since ancient times resulting in two types of modern mango cultivars: the "Indian type" and the "Southeast Asian type". Other species in the genus Mangifera also produce edible fruits that are also called "mangoes", the majority of which are found in the Malesian ecoregion.

MUSK MELON

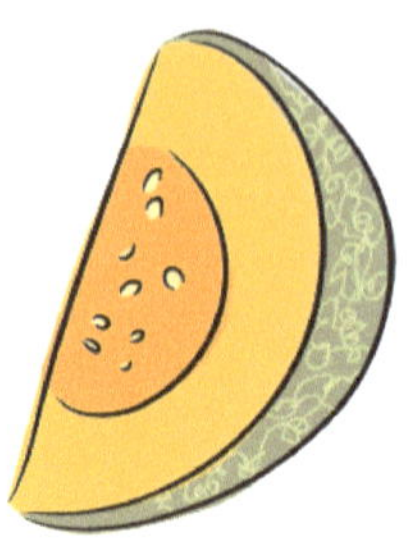

Cucumis melo, also known as melon, is a species of Cucumis that has been developed into many cultivated varieties. The fruit is a pepo. The flesh is either sweet or bland, with or without a musky aroma, and the rind can be smooth (such as honeydew), ribbed (such as cantaloupe), wrinkled (such as casaba melon), or netted (such as muskmelon). In North America, the sweet-flesh varieties are often collectively called muskmelon, including the musky netted-rind varieties and the inodorous smooth-rind varieties, and cantaloupe usually means the former type.

ORANGE

An orange is a fruit of various citrus species in the family Rutaceae (see list of plants known as orange); it primarily refers to Citrus × sinensis, which is also called sweet orange, to distinguish it from the related Citrus × aurantium, referred to as bitter orange. The sweet orange reproduces asexually (apomixis through nucellar embryony); varieties of sweet orange arise through mutations.

PAPAYA

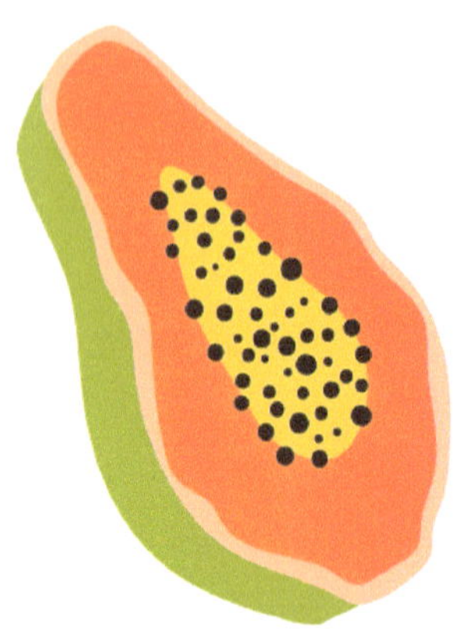

The papaya (/pəˈpaɪə/, US: /pəˈpɑːjə/) (from Carib via Spanish), papaw, (/pəˈpɔː/) or pawpaw (/ˈpɔːpɔː/) is the plant Carica papaya, one of the 22 accepted species in the genus Carica of the family Caricaceae. It was first domesticated in Mesoamerica, within modern-day southern Mexico and Central America. In 2020, India produced 43% of the world supply of papayas.

PEACH

This fuzzy fruit is the pride and joy of the South. Peaches are baked in desserts, served with ice cream and mixed into jams. If you don't have access to fresh peaches, don't worry! Canned unpeeled peaches have similar amounts of vitamins and minerals – just make sure there is no added sugar.

Good source of vitamin C and A.
Packed with antioxidants.
Contains both soluble and insoluble fiber.

PEAR

This sweet and crunchy snack comes in a variety of colors and shapes. Pears can be enjoyed fresh, cooked in cinnamon or baked into desserts. Though not particularly high in any specific nutrient, the pear boasts a range of micronutrients.

Outstanding source of vitamin C and vitamin K.
Contains copper, potassium and manganese.

PINEAPPLE

The pineapple (Ananas comosus) is a tropical plant with an edible fruit; it is the most economically significant plant in the family Bromeliaceae. The pineapple is indigenous to South America, where it has been cultivated for many centuries. The introduction of the pineapple to Europe in the 17th century made it a significant cultural icon of luxury. Since the 1820s, pineapple has been commercially grown in greenhouses and many tropical plantations.

POMEGRANATE

The pomegranate (Punica granatum) is a fruit-bearing deciduous shrub in the family Lythraceae, subfamily Punicoideae, that grows between 5 and 10 m (16 and 33 ft) tall.

The pomegranate was originally described throughout the Mediterranean region. It was introduced into Spanish America in the late 16th century and into California by Spanish settlers in 1769.

STRAWBERRY

The garden strawberry (or simply strawberry; Fragaria × ananassa) is a widely grown hybrid species of the genus Fragaria, collectively known as the strawberries, which are cultivated worldwide for their fruit. The fruit is widely appreciated for its characteristic aroma, bright red color, juicy texture, and sweetness. It is consumed in large quantities, either fresh or in such prepared foods as jam, juice, pies, ice cream, milkshakes, and chocolates. Artificial strawberry flavorings and aromas are also widely used in products such as candy, soap, lip gloss, perfume, and many others.

WATERMELON

Watermelon (Citrullus lanatus) is a flowering plant species of the Cucurbitaceae family and the name of its edible fruit. A scrambling and trailing vine-like plant, it is a highly cultivated fruit worldwide, with more than 1,000 varieties.

FRUITS NAMES

Apples
Apricots
Avocados
Bananas
Boysenberries
Blueberries
Bing Cherry
Cherries
Cantaloupe
Crab apples
Clementine
Cucumbers
Damson plum
Dinosaur Eggs
Dates
Dewberries
Dragon
Elderberry
Eggfruit
Evergreen
Huckleberry

Entawak
Fig
Farkleberry
Finger Lime
Grapefruit
Grapes
Gooseberries
Guava
Honeydew melon
Hackberry
Honeycrisp Apples
Indian Prune
Indonesian Lime
Imbe
Indian Fig
Jackfruit
Java Apple
Jambolan
Kiwi
Kaffir Lime
Kumquat

Lime
Longan
Lychee
Loquat
Mango
Mandarin
Orange
Mulberry
Melon
Nectarine
Navel Orange
Nashi Pear
Olive
Oranges
Ogeechee Limes
Oval Kumquat
Papaya
Persimmon
Paw Paw
Prickly Pear
Peach
Pomegranate
Pineapple

Passion Fruit
Quince
Queen Anne Cherry
Quararibea cordata
Rambutan
Raspberries
Rose Hips
Star Fruit
Strawberries
Sugar Baby
Watermelon
Tomato
Tangerine
Tamarind
Tart Cherries
Uniq Fruit
Ugni
Vanilla Bean
Velvet Pink Banana
Watermelon
Xigua
Yangmei
Zucchini

www.ingramcontent.com/pod-product-compliance
Lightning Source LLC
LaVergne TN
LVHW071219160826
845679LV00003B/872

9798846081093